HOW TO WRITE A J

Bernard Ungerson, CBE, has retired from a distinguished career in industrial psychology and personnel management. The posts and offices he has held include Chief Psychologist at the War Office, Chairman of the Occupational Psychology Section of the British Psychological Society, Chairman of the Staff Management Association, President of the Institute of Personnel Management and Head of Personnel in both national and multinational groups of companies. He is a Fellow of the British Psychological Society and Honorary Life Companion of the Institute of Personnel Management.

How to Write a Job Description

Bernard Ungerson

INSTITUTE OF PERSONNEL MANAGEMENT

Note: the convention has been followed whereby *he* and *him* are used to cover *she* and *her* whenever appropriate. This should not be taken to denote any sex preference or priority.

First published 1983
© *Institute of Personnel Management 1983*
Reprinted 1986

All rights reserved
Unauthorized duplication contravenes applicable laws

British Library Cataloguing in Publication Data
Ungerson, Bernard
   How to write a job description.
   1. Work design
   I. Title
   658.3'06   T60.8

ISBN 0-85292-268-X

Printed in Great Britain by
Latimer Trend & Company Ltd, Plymouth

Contents

General objectives and outline		1
1	Job descriptions and the line manager	3
2	Some preliminary issues	5
	Job descriptions should be simple	5
	Job descriptions should not overstate or exaggerate	5
	Job descriptions should not be confused with job specifications	6
3	How job descriptions fit into the management process	7
4	Job descriptions and staff development	9
5	The value of job descriptions	11
	For the organization	11
	For the individual	13
6	How should job descriptions be produced?	14
	By whom?	14
	Raising problems	15

7	The content of job descriptions	16
	The job title	16
	To whom the individual reports	16
	For whom the individual is directly responsible	17
	Overall purpose of the job	17
	Key result areas: desirability	18
	Key result areas: content	19
	Specific objectives and standards for the coming period	21
8	Training, overlap and consistency	24
9	Top management, flexibility and updating	26
10	Job descriptions for shop-floor jobs?	29
11	Incapability, dismissals and industrial tribunals	30
12	Some satisfactory examples	32
13	Examples of what to avoid	50
	Index	63

General objectives and outline

The title may suggest that this publication is concerned only with recording existing tasks and standards. It will however also deal with important wider issues. Writing job descriptions necessarily involves discussions and changes. It also can help to develop a favourable atmosphere for the joint solution of problems. The process should be inter-linked with corporate planning (which exists informally, even if there is no specific function for the purpose). It should also be linked with staff development and especially with appraisal interviewing.

All these matters are discussed in detail below. A preliminary outline of the major points may, however, be useful.

The objective of a job description is to record the facts about the job content. These should include the job title, reporting relationships upward and downward, the overall purpose of the job, a short description of the main activities, arranged in 'key result areas'.

The job description should be simple, should not exaggerate and should not be confused with a job specification. It should fit in with corporate planning and with staff development.

It should be drafted by the job holder (if competent) and agreed by more senior management. Specialists can help but should not usurp the line managers' role.

Job descriptions can and should be used for the benefit of both the organization and the job holder. They serve the organization by providing:

a definition of individual tasks

a basis for reviewing performance

a basis for job specifications

a basis for reviewing organization structure

a basis for establishing job grades

a basis for arranging appropriate training

support in dealing with incapability, dismissals and industrial tribunals.

For the job-holder they provide:

a knowledge of what is expected and of the standards by which he will be judged

an opportunity to take part in setting standards

an opportunity to resolve problems.

All concerned need training, especially to ensure consistency throughout the organization. Job descriptions should apply to all jobs right up to the top. Exceptionally, there may often be a case for excluding the shop floor if adequate descriptions exist for special purposes such as job evaluation.

1
Job descriptions and the line manager

Job descriptions are often written because personnel departments think they are 'a good idea' but without line managers' commitment to their value. This merely ensures that a paper exercise is pushed through and that dust then gathers on piles of paper whose contents become rapidly out of date.

To avoid this, there must be clear ideas of what the job descriptions are to be used for and these ideas must be 'sold' to line managers before the exercise starts. This is not easy and is even less so in the many organizations which already possess the results of previous attempts—unused and out of date. Nevertheless, the preparatory selling is vital. Job descriptions, like all other products and activities of the personnel function must be useful to line managers and be seen by them to contribute to efficiency and profit or they will fail in their purpose.

This, in turn, means that personnel departments must be quite clear about how the job descriptions are to be used. If this is not clear, and if the uses are not important, it is best not to embark on the exercise. For it will achieve nothing except justified criticism of personnel departments.

It is vital that the line managers should feel (correctly) that they have played the major part in preparing the job descriptions.

To this end, and because they are most competent to do the work accurately, line managers must play the most important part in the discussions, in the guidance during drafting, and in checking and authorizing the final versions. They must also be closely concerned with the changes which result from the discussion and agreement of job descriptions.

Lastly, line managers are key figures in avoiding or preventing overlap and duplication. This important matter is discussed in chapter 8. The result of every job description should be a statement which distinguishes that particular job from all other jobs in the organization.

2

Some preliminary issues

1 JOB DESCRIPTIONS SHOULD BE SIMPLE

Many job descriptions are so complex that the mere sight of them causes line managers to turn against them. The common separation of such areas as 'duties', 'authorities', 'responsibilities', 'accountabilities', and so on leads to complexity. Experience suggests that such divisions, while theoretically valid, are an unnecessary complication. Job descriptions should concentrate on *actions*. For a responsibility cannot be met unless the individual takes the necessary actions to carry it out; for example, regular checking of output quality or material consumption. Similarly, an authority cannot be exercised by psychic forces. The authority requires *actions*, or it is not exercised adequately.

Other sources of complexity are verbiage, repetition and muddled syntax. Every idea, every statement and, indeed, every word must be made to 'fight for its life'. It is common to find that first drafts can be edited down, with no loss of content, to half their original length. This helps greatly in getting them read and accepted.

2 JOB DESCRIPTIONS SHOULD NOT OVERSTATE OR EXAGGERATE

It is common experience that, once line managers settle down to discuss and agree job descriptions, they frequently tend to exaggerate the importance and the multiplicity of the duties. This is done partly by writing in as many petty duties as possible and partly by the use of inflated wording to overstate the duties. Thus 'files' may become 'controls, issues and maintains correspondence both incoming and outgoing, plus other varied documentation'.

The reasons for such overstatements are known only to their authors but empire-building and self-glorification no doubt play their parts. Also where wages, salary scales or job grades are dependent upon job content, by means of job evaluation, there are frequently efforts to justify higher evaluations by overstated job descriptions.

The remedy for this lies primarily in using the simple, systematic approach recommended below. If abstract nouns, ill-defined phrases, inexact statements and high-flown phraseology are allowed, it is difficult to disprove exaggerated statements. But where terse, factual, active phrases are used, in an orderly fashion and arranged in 'key result areas', it becomes much more difficult for over-statement to survive the discussion process.

3 JOB DESCRIPTIONS SHOULD NOT BE CONFUSED WITH JOB SPECIFICATIONS

It is essential to remember the difference between these two and to keep them separate. The job description is intended to describe the work necessary to carry out the job effectively; the job specification is intended to set out the characteristics of the individual (intelligence, aptitudes, training etc) required to do the job. These are very different objectives and the two documents are necessarily set out in different terms. The job description is best set out in key result areas; the job specification needs some framework such as the NIIP 7 point plan.

Many job descriptions contain an ill-assorted mixture of the two sorts of information and, as a consequence, are confused and confusing. This is a negation of the simplicity of layout and content which are essential if job descriptions are to be accepted and used.

Throughout this publication the term 'job specification' is used for the statement of characteristics of the job-holder required to perform the job satisfactorily. The term has the same meaning as 'person specification' which is now tending to replace it.

3

How job descriptions fit into the management process

The description of an individual job must take into account the objectives of the organization as a whole. If it does not, the job description may set objectives and standards which are unnecessary or irrelevant. Or, on the other hand it may leave out some objectives which are essential to fulfil the plans.

It follows that job descriptions must be associated with the corporate planning of the organization, company or group. The total process is a hierarchy of plans, like this (for a group of companies):

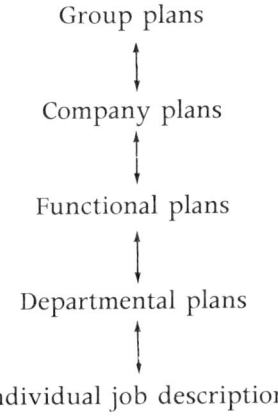

In practice, the upper planning levels can be left to those responsible for corporate planning. The practical step for writers of job descriptions is to check that they meet, accurately, the needs of the departmental plans. These should exist in a well-run organization but, if not, the best that can be done is to ensure that each job description, at the final draft stage, is seen and passed by the appropriate manager at the next level up.

4

Job descriptions and staff development

If job descriptions are to be realistic and are not to duplicate work being done elsewhere, they should be part of the process of developing and training the human resources of the organization.

To see this as a unified whole, it is necessary to see how the various parts of the process fit together. This is shown in the following diagram:

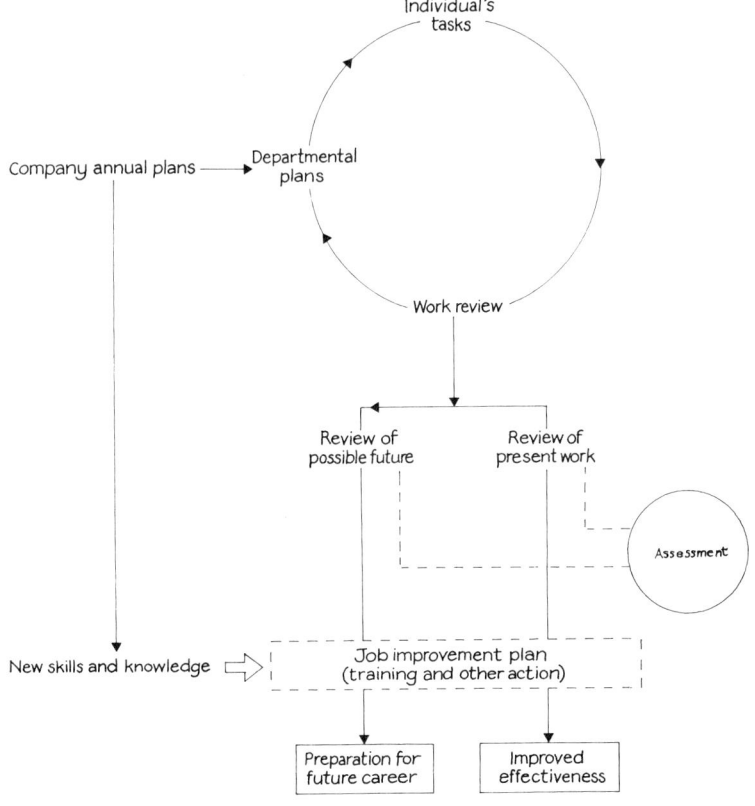

It can be seen (top left) that the company's annual plans lead to the discussion and agreement of departmental plans. It is only after this that the jobs of individuals can be realistically discussed and recorded. The individual's tasks include both the continuing objectives and the specific objectives for the coming period. When these tasks are reviewed, the complete job description should be discussed, improvements agreed and objectives and targets set. At the end of the period the work review (commonly and unfortunately known as the appraisal interview) can take place. It is during these procedures that the job description should be reconsidered and updated as necessary.

The diagram also shows how the work review should lead to improved effectiveness. This is the major characteristic which should ensure that the job description is of practical value and that this is appreciated by the line manager. Unless the link between the job description and effectiveness in practice is strong, it will be seen—quite rightly—as a paper exercise without relevance to the real aims and problems of the organization. If, on the contrary, it deals with real problems and helps to solve them, it will be valued by the line manager who will help rather than resist.

5

The value of job descriptions

This is best assessed by considering what needs they can usefully meet, for the organization and for the individual.

1 FOR THE ORGANIZATION

The organization should derive the following benefits from producing job descriptions:

An effective means of defining each individual's tasks

This has great value in promoting efficiency and smooth working practices. But it also has a powerful influence in preventing what are often seen as clashes of personality. For many of these clashes are, in reality, due to lack of clear definitions of the margins of responsibility. This can lead either to 'he is intruding or interfering in my job' or, on the other hand, 'why blame me for neglecting it?—I thought it was his job'.

A basis on which to review performance

It is clear that no-one's performance can be adequately reviewed without objectives and standards which were agreed at the beginning of the review period. Anything else is unfair and is liable, rightly, to lead to defensive arguments as to whether the objective or standard had been made clear and explicit to the person under review.

A good clear job description, on the other hand, can help enormously with one of management's trickiest problems *viz* carrying out appraisal interviews or, to use a much better title, work review discussions. It is well known that many managers dislike these, find them very difficult and avoid or skimp them as far as possible. The job description can play an important part in overcoming the tensions and difficulties which tend to frighten managers off. A direct attack upon strengths and weaknesses can be avoided as far as possible and replaced by a discussion of the work content, concentrating upon avoiding past difficulties in the future, the interviewee's suggestions for improved effectiveness and so on. The job description can act as an agenda for such a discussion, taking out some of the heat engendered by personality issues and ensuring that all major areas of the job are properly discussed.

A basis for a job specification

A clear job description is essential before a job specification can be prepared. It is not possible to decide the aptitudes, skills, knowledge and other personal qualities required for a job unless its objectives and content have been considered and clearly recorded. The job description thus plays an important part in all recruitment, transfer or promotion decisions.

A basis for reviewing its organization structure

When a job description is written, there has to be detailed discussion of job content. This always raises questions about organization structure, for many of the difficulties and doubts of individuals are found to stem from an unclear or unsatisfactory organization structure. The writing, and regular revision, of job descriptions therefore leads to a necessary and regular critical survey of organization structure. If this is unclear, unsatisfactory or in need of change, the job description process is very likely to draw attention to what is the problem.

A basis for establishing and updating job grades

Whatever method of job grading is used, it is essential to be clear about job content, objectives and standards. This information is best provided by a clear job description.

A basis for adequate training

Training for any job should ensure that the job-holder acquires the skills and knowledge necessary to carry out all essential elements of the job competently. It should also avoid wasting time and effort on anything which is irrelevant or trivial. These two requirements are best met by working systematically through a properly drafted job description.

2 For the individual

So much for the needs of the organization. What does the individual need? This is not easy to answer, for individuals differ in their wishes and attitudes. But it seems likely that there are sufficient similarities to suggest that an individual needs the following:

To know what is expected of him

This is self-evident. Any individual who does not know this is likely to exceed requirements in some respects and fail to meet them in others. The resulting difficulties and likely criticisms and conflicts can lead only to self-doubts, lack of confidence and inefficiency. Criticisms will often come as a surprise and be regarded as unfair. It is only right that the individual should know the standards by which he will be judged.

An opportunity to take part in setting his tasks and standards

If the individual plays a part in writing his own job description (as is suggested below), he can be involved in ensuring that these are reasonable and attainable. Naturally, full agreement cannot always be reached easily but given a reasonable approach by all concerned, acceptable tasks and standards can normally be agreed.

An opportunity to discuss and resolve problems outside his own control

This is perhaps the most important benefit to be derived from writing job descriptions. If they are prepared by the discussion process recommended in chapter 6, problems which lower efficiency are bound to come to light, to the benefit of the individual and the organization. Often this leads to improvement. This, in turn, ensures that the job description records not just present practice but new improved practices.

This sort of discussion not only leads to improvement in efficiency; it can do much to raise the morale of the individual and improve the quality and effectiveness of management.

6

How should job descriptions be produced?

1 BY WHOM?

It is undesirable that job descriptions should be written and imposed upon the job-holder by a manager or other senior person. In this process, as in all management situations, participation is likely to make the process and the final product more acceptable to all concerned.

Neither is it good practice for 'specialists' to produce them, working in isolation. This is not to say that specialists have no role to play in achieving good job descriptions. They can, and should, train line managers and they can cooperate with those who need help. But this should be done in such a way as to leave the main responsibility with the job-holder and his/her immediate superior.

The best arrangement is for the job-holder to be directly involved in preparing his/her own description. Unless he/she is completely incapable of making a reasonable try at the task, no-one else should intervene between giving preliminary guidance and, later, discussing the first draft.

There are thus two possibilities, each involving three levels.

The first, and best, is for the job-holder to prepare a draft and discuss and agree it with his/her immediate superior. Then, in order to ensure that it fits harmoniously into broader plans, it should be seen and approved by the superior's immediate boss.

The alternative, if the job-holder is not able to prepare a draft without help, is for him and his superior to prepare and agree the draft together and then for it to be approved at the next level up.

If this arrangement is used, everything possible must be done to maximize the contribution of the job-holder.

2   Raising problems

During the process of drafting and discussing, the job-holder should raise any problems which decrease his effectiveness and which he cannot deal with himself. Such problems may include:

- inappropriate or unclear organization objectives
- insufficient resources in people, equipment or otherwise
- insufficient, inadequate, irrelevant or late information
- need for training to carry out the agreed tasks effectively
- inadequate help or co-operation from other departments or individuals.

With all matters of such kinds he can, and should, obtain the help of his senior.

This process is, in practice, highly beneficial. It is sometimes objected that problems should not await the discussion and writing of a job description. This is, of course, true and the process suggested is not intended, and must not be allowed, to replace the day to day handling of problems and constant striving for greater effectiveness.

But experience shows that the continuous process and the general attack on all problems through the discussion of job descriptions can go hand-in-hand. However smoothly problems appear to be handled as they arise, there are always many which operatives and managers are 'too busy to bother with today'. It is common experience that 'the urgent drives out the important', ie that fire-fighting takes priority over planned improvement. Those who have worked on job descriptions in the ways suggested find that many problems, of which people have been more or less aware, are brought into focus, studied, discussed and solved. This can be, and usually is, entirely beneficial. The whole process has extremely good training and development effects upon all concerned.

7

The content of job descriptions

Job descriptions normally record objectives and tasks. These are general and stable from period to period unless there are changes within the organization or in the allocation of work to individuals. Some job descriptions also include specific objectives and standards for the immediate future. These are more detailed and tend to arise from new or expanded needs, from deficiencies which need to be overcome or from requirements for improved effectiveness. There are pros and cons for including these in the job description and they are considered in section 7 on page 21.

The following are the suggested sections of an adequate but simple and straightforward job description.

1 THE JOB TITLE

This should, as far as possible, be a realistic description of the job. There is little to be said for giving jobs grandiloquent titles in order to gratify individuals. It should also be remembered that the status of jobs may be publicly assumed to be equal if they have the same title. There may sometimes be a case for allotting exaggerated titles if recruitment would be assisted (it may be possible to recruit, say, 'boiler technicians' when stokers are in short supply). But, in general, titles should remain realistic. There is no point in giving the title of 'manager' to employees who manage nobody.

2 TO WHOM THE INDIVIDUAL REPORTS

This is often, but not always, clear and simple. Complications can arise. In one example, the general manager of a very large nationalized enterprise in a developing country began by saying that he was responsible to 'the National Corporation'. When it was pointed out that this was hardly possible since chaos would inevitably follow if instructions could be given by about 12 people, the general manager suggested he was responsible to the high-ranking politician who had appointed him. Discussion of all this led to a clarification of the general relations between the organization, the National Corporation and the politicians, with benefits throughout the whole pyramid.

There are many cases in which individuals, asked 'to whom do you report?', answer vaguely or in such terms as 'partly to A and partly to B' or 'to A for quality and to B for everything else'. Such situations need to be sorted out before writing a job description can begin. Thus, this first, apparently simple, piece of recording can give warning of fundamental weaknesses or muddles in the organization.

3 For whom the individual is directly responsible

This should record only those at the next level down and no lower. There is a danger of this being misunderstood. For example, a departmental superintendent may say 'I am responsible for 70 people', including everybody in 'his' department. In reality he is directly responsible only for, say, four foremen, one or two staff specialists and a clerical assistant.

Problems similar to those described in the previous section can arise, especially in cases of split or joint responsibility. These, again, should be sorted out before the job description is written.

4 Overall purpose of the job

It is useful to have a brief statement of this. It can be written at an early stage, but it is perhaps better left until the detailed main body of the job description has been discussed, agreed and written. Without this, there can be mistaken ideas of the main work areas. For example, in a recent updating of a job description it was found that 60 per cent of the working week was spent on one activity which had been so little appreciated that it was not previously mentioned in the statement of overall purpose of the job.

5 Key result areas: desirability

These constitute the main body of the job description. They are vitally important since they help with clear thinking and they provide headings and subdivisions to make the job description readable. Many job descriptions are produced without them and are consequently deficient in completeness, clarity and presentation.

It is common to see job descriptions with 30, 40 or more separate items, not arranged in any rational order. Such a format is a guarantee of muddled thinking, with repetitions, overlaps and omissions. Moreover, the final result cannot be comprehended in any logical way and tends to nonplus the reader. To mix the metaphors, such job descriptions look an indigestible mass in which the wood cannot be seen for the trees. It is very much better to have up to about 10 key result areas, each with its clear heading, to tell the reader exactly what each main area is and to forewarn him of each topic in orderly fashion.

It is true, moreover, that the process of collecting the various individual activities into 'key areas' helps to clarify thinking, to simplify and to avoid duplication or omissions. The following is an example of the key result area headings for a marketing manager:

Sales force management

Collecting and interpreting market information

Monitoring customer satisfaction

Pricing policy

Sales promotion

Advertising

Information for production and technical divisions

Budgeting, planning and control

Training and developing staff

Setting up such headings will ensure that the main body of the job description is clearly and logically framed. All depends, however, upon what is written under each heading. This is discussed in the next section.

6 KEY RESULT AREAS: CONTENT

In order to achieve clarity and to ensure that the job description is as useful as possible, the following are recommended:

(i) Under each heading, each sub-paragraph should use active nouns rather than abstractions. Phrases such as 'liaison with', 'keep in contact with', 'frequent inspection of' are all too vague or inexact to be worth using.

(ii) Objectives should, whenever possible, be quantified in terms of such factors as cost, output, wastage, speed or time.

(iii) The wording should distinguish between those activities which are to be carried out by the job-holder and those which she/he has to see that others carry out. The former is a direct working responsibility; the latter is a managerial responsibility. The best word for such managerial responsibility is 'ensure', for that is what a good manager ought to do. This usually implies that the manager
   (a) ensures that all concerned are properly selected, trained and informed about standards required
   (b) monitors, at agreed fixed intervals, either by inspection or by means of appropriate management information
   (c) takes remedial action.

Usually, the first draft of a job description, written by the job-holder, will contain a number of vague generalizations. Let us see how such a generalization can be made clear and precise.

The draft for a departmental superintendent may read:

'Responsible for the quality of output'

The discussion could go along the following lines:

'But do you personally make the product?'
'Well, no.'
'Then how can you be responsible for quality?'
'Well, I am responsible.'
'Okay I accept that. But how do you do it?'

'I have to see to it that the workers maintain the necessary standards.'

'I see, so you have to "ensure that the department's output is of the required standard".'

'That's right.'

'How do you do it? There seems to be two questions;

(i) where are the standards laid down for you and the department? and

(ii) how do you "ensure" that they are reached?'

'The standards are recorded in the addendums to the drawings.'

'Are these available to the operatives?'

'No, not really.'

'Would you agree that it would help with quality if they had this information?'

'Yes.'

'Well, then we'll have to deal with that when we discuss their job descriptions. Also, we'll have to include in yours that you should ensure that the operatives have, and understand, the information about quality standards.

Now, how are you going to monitor the quality of output?'

'Well I keep an eye on it as I go round.'

'That's fine. But is there any way in which you can introduce a regular drill for this monitoring? Can it perhaps be done from any return or form?'

'Yes. It might be possible from the computer returns on raw material wastage of the figures kept by the inspectors.'

This sort of discussion can lead to a valuable tightening up of the methods of quality control. The original vague statement 'responsible for the quality of output' is finally replaced by:

1 PRODUCTION
1.1 *Quality*
Ensure that output is of the required standard. To achieve this:
(i) Provide all operatives with quality standards and inspect on the first Monday of each month to ensure these are available, understood and used.

- (ii) Personally carry out a visual inspection of output at least once per week.
- (iii) Monitor the weekly inspection department return (ID7), investigate cases where rejection exceeds x per cent and take remedial action by guidance, training, warning or otherwise.

This detailed record of *actions* is a far cry from the original 'pious hope' and is almost certain to bring about a significant improvement in the department's quality of output. If existing job descriptions are examined critically in the same way, similar improvements can, in most cases, be made. But perhaps even more important than the final product is the approach, the discussion and the changes which result. Anyone who has to participate in writing or rewriting job descriptions should look carefully at each item and ask:

- (i) Does it clearly separate direct personal actions from those which have to be carried out by subordinates or other people?
- (ii) If the latter, is there a built-in process of regular monitoring and/or inspection?
- (iii) Is adequate regular information available to the job-holder to enable him to monitor performance?
- (iv) Does it use crisp active verbs, calling for action, rather than vague abstractions?
- (v) Does it contain only continuing, stable objectives, and leave short-term, specific non-recurring objectives to the separate list of objectives and standards for the coming period?

If these simple questions are applied they will help greatly towards initiating a process of valuable job improvement and clearly recording the outcome, in a clear, terse job description.

7   Specific objectives and standards for the coming period

These are all the agreed actions and objectives which are not repeated identically year after year but which are single actions to be carried out or objectives to be achieved within the coming period.

It is a matter of opinion and convenience whether they are regarded as part of the job description or as a separate record. If the continuing objectives (the major section of the job description) are discussed systematically at a work review discussion, as recommended above, a great many proposed short-term actions and objectives will be agreed. These can be recorded either as part of the job description, alongside the relevant key result areas (KRAs) or, if more convenient, as a separate document.

If the former arrangement is preferred, it is best to arrange the job description in two major columns with headings as shown in the following example. This has the advantage that the continuing objectives and the corresponding specific short-term objectives are side by side. It has the disadvantage that the whole of the job description has to be reproduced, even if there are no changes to the left-hand side (the continuing objectives).

Key result areas and continuing objectives

There are probably up to 10 KRAs, or main divisions of a person's job, in which it is essential that he obtains results.

Consider the overall purpose of your job and identify the KRAs in each of which you must obtain results if you are to play an effective part in achieving your department's objectives.

List each KRA and below each describe the general objectives which you must seek to achieve.

Specific job objectives

Consider each KRA separately. Take account of your department's objectives and state, briefly, the specific objectives which you must aim to achieve during the next review period. If there are none in any KRA write NONE.

Whenever possible set the standards which will describe when

each objective has been carried out satisfactorily, assuming normal working conditions eg
Time—By what time?
Cost—Within what cost?
Quantity—How much?
Quality—How well?

Key result areas and continuing objectives	Specific job objectives
1 SALES FORCE MANAGEMENT	
1.1 From the sales forecasts, calculate the sales and continuously monitor the sales force required over the following 12 months period.	
1.2 Ensure, by training and development, or by recruitment, that sufficient trained salesmen are always available to meet the department's needs.	By 30 September recruit or promote two additional salesmen, within the agreed salary range; plan individual induction and/or development programmes for each. Report progress to the Sales Director on 1 August and 1 September.
1.3 Report briefly in writing, once every three months, to the sales director on the requirements for and supply of salesmen.	

8

Training, overlap and consistency

It is essential that job descriptions should be clear and as short as possible. It is also important that the same general format and style should be used throughout an organization and that there should be no overlap or duplication of responsibilities. Consistency of format is desirable for general reasons but is particularly important if job descriptions are used as part of a job evaluation procedure. If formats differ greatly, comparative assessments become virtually impossible.

These ends will not be achieved without proper training of all concerned and some system of guidance during the drafting process and checking of the final drafts. This is best done by a specialist adviser. As suggested in section 6 on page 14, the actual drafting should not be done by a specialist but his contribution to training, guidance, co-ordination and checking will be vital.

The specialist can be an external expert or, perhaps preferably, a reasonably senior member of the personnel function who has himself been trained and experienced in the preparation of job descriptions.

The specialist will need to maintain a balance between interfering too little or too much. On the one hand, as stressed above, the line managers must feel, rightly, that job descriptions are primarily their own responsibility. On the other hand, they must be sufficiently trained and guided to ensure consistency and avoid overlap.

This has to be achieved within individual departments and also among the different departments. The former is best ensured by each department head. He, if properly trained, should spot undesirable differences of format and duplications or contradictions among his own subordinates. He should also be on the look out for situations where the content of one job description necessitates addition, deletion or alteration to another job description within his own area of responsibility.

It is rather more complex to achieve the same ends among various departments. In theory, the same process could be followed. All that is necessary is to move up the hierarchy and have a more senior manager guide and cross-check to ensure consistency and lack of duplication among two or more departments. In practice, this is unlikely to work satisfactorily. Senior managers are unlikely to be prepared to study, in detail, the job descriptions of people two or more levels lower than themselves. It is more likely that the specialist adviser (internal or external) will be prepared and able to carry out this important co-ordinating role. And it is vital that it should be carried out.

9

Top management, flexibility and updating

Three criticisms are often made of job descriptions. These are:

(i) that job descriptions are not appropriate for top management because these people should be free to map out their own territory, show initiative and so on

(ii) that job descriptions are a hindrance to the development of organizations which are growing rapidly or changing technologically. It is argued that job descriptions are too inflexible for such conditions and that they slow down or even prevent desirable changes to meet new conditions

(iii) that, because there is always 'drift' in job content, job descriptions become out of date very quickly and are therefore ignored: at any rate until some major problem or catastrophe causes them to be reconsidered and redrafted.

The answer to all these criticisms lies in making appropriate arrangements for updating. To reject job descriptions because of the fears described above is to throw out the baby with the bathwater.

Consider each criticism in turn.

1 Top management

Lack of clarity in the areas of responsibility at top level can, and often does, have more serious consequences than at lower levels. There can be few more serious threats to the effectiveness of an organization than this kind of uncertainty. Moreover, the uncertainty inevitably spreads 'down the line'. As explained above, each individual job description must harmonize with plans and job descriptions at the next level up. If, at the top, there are no job descriptions, then those of the top executives just below board level will not be anchored in reality. This will then weaken the framework for those at the next level down and so on. It follows that job descriptions should start at the top. This is not easy to achieve for it is common experience that directors often take the view that 'it's all right for them but it obviously doesn't apply to us'. Nevertheless, every effort should be made to persuade directors to conform. Their wishes for freedom should be met by building flexibility into the structure and wording of their job descriptions. There should also be arrangements for regular updating and for additional updating whenever changes make this necessary.

2 FLEXIBILITY

Much the same is true of the need for flexibility to meet the changing circumstances caused by rapid growth or technological change. It is true that changes are likely to occur irregularly and that it is not easy to ensure that the necessary changes in job descriptions are made immediately, although this is the ideal. Here, again, therefore, regular updating is the main answer. This updating will be virtually guaranteed if, as suggested above, the job description is used as an 'agenda' for regular work review discussions. As each key result area is discussed, any need for updating is inevitably revealed.

It should perhaps be added that there should not necessarily be a strict adherence to annual work review discussions and the resulting updating of job descriptions. It is likely that, in jobs subject to rapid growth or change, the discussions should be more frequent.

3 UPDATING

Finally, the same principles apply to 'drift' in job content. The remedy is not to abandon job descriptions but to ensure that updating takes place regularly and on a time-scale to meet the circumstances of each job situation.

In short, the criticisms can be valid if appropriate steps are not taken to meet them. But if such steps are taken, job descriptions can overcome the potential difficulties and prove especially beneficial.

10

Job descriptions for shop-floor jobs?

At first glance it might appear desirable that all shop-floor jobs should have job descriptions along the same lines as management, supervisory and staff jobs. But deeper consideration suggests that this is not so.

There appear to be good reasons why few organizations have job descriptions as an end in themselves. Many do however have recorded analyses of jobs for special purposes. The most common of these is job evaluation, which has led many organizations to record analyses of shop-floor jobs for the first time. Other forms of job analysis often exist for work measurement, for training and for technical/design reasons (setting out dimensions, tolerances etc). It seems likely that most organizations are unwilling to add to one or more of these records yet another paper exercise. Personnel departments would be unwise to press for job descriptions in addition to these other records unless they can achieve adequate coordination and avoid duplication.

There are two important points to add.

First, the form of any job description or similar record must be decided primarily by the requirements of the system of job evaluation, work measurement or training which is in use or proposed and with which it must harmonize.

Secondly, there may be industrial relations implications which should be carefully considered. Job descriptions for shop-floor jobs may, only too easily, be used to establish demarcation boundaries and to resist desirable changes in work methods and organization. These problems, serious as they are, go beyond the scope of this publication, but it would be perilous to ignore them.

11

Incapability, dismissals and industrial tribunals

Handling employees who are found to be incapable always presents a personnel problem. It also, nowadays, presents legal problems if dismissal is finally unavoidable and may have to be defended at an industrial tribunal. Good job descriptions can help with both the personnel and the legal aspects.

The ideal, of course, is to avoid the development of incapability. This is best achieved by:

careful selection and recruitment

clear communication of tasks and standards

thorough training

regular work reviews

In all of these, job descriptions should play a vital part, as emphasized in chapters 3, 4, 5 and 7.

If it becomes necessary to consider, and finally to decide upon, dismissal, this is likely to be ruled as unfair unless there has been, in addition to the necessary warnings, time to improve and feedback during the improvement period:

clear statement of the job requirements and standards

training in all parts of the job and especially those in which the job-holder is found incapable.

In both of these matters, a clear, agreed job description will not only ensure justice and a reasonable chance to the job-holder but is likely to play a large part in convincing a tribunal that the dismissal is fair.

12

Some satisfactory examples

This chapter contains examples of job descriptions set out generally in the way recommended above. None of them is perfect. There are some breaches, in all of them, of the suggested general principles. There are examples of excessive verbiage, of lack of clarity, of failure to build in monitoring or to quantify objectives where this is desirable and possible. But comparison with many published examples does show, perhaps encouragingly, that they are clearer, simpler, less prolix and more to the point than many, if not most. The reader, in picking the deficiencies in these examples may well develop an ability to criticize constructively which will serve him well in drafting, or helping others to draft, job descriptions.

EXAMPLE 1

This is for the Chief Executive of a very large industrial company which has recently become part of a major holding company. The job description has to clarify the organizational relationship between this company and the holding company, which can be expressed satisfactorily in terms of responsibilities and the upward reporting relationship of the Chief Executive. It also has to record clearly the actions which he has to take and those which he delegates, with arrangements for monitoring and taking any necessary remedial action. When this job description was drafted, the company was in an early stage of being co-ordinated into the group. It is therefore in rather more general terms than are normally desirable. As relationships develop and are clarified, the various actions will come to refer more precisely to the procedures and documents used in planning, controlling and reporting.

Example 2

This is a somewhat unusual job which combines a normal salesman's function with responsibility for recruitment (subject to final decision at a higher level) and for the induction and training of sales trainees. There is also some involvement in development work.

The major characteristic is that these varied responsibilities are clearly separated by the use of KRAs. Also, it is made clear what are the limits below which the job holder may, and should, make decisions. This applies to sales matters such as estimating and invoicing, and to recruitment.

Example 3

This is a straightforward job description of a senior clerical job. Many of the activities should be monitored and the actions necessary for this are included in the job description of the librarian, to whom this job-holder reports.

Example 4

This is a clear example of a high level accounts job. It could be further improved by building in the actions to be taken to monitor the many duties which the job-holder has to 'ensure'. Questions about the procedures, their frequency and regularity, could usefully be asked about section 3 'Costing', for example. The answers would do much to make the job description a more powerful control document.

Nevertheless, the example, as it stands, is clearer and more precise than many.

Example 5

This is for a straightforward salesman's job and calls for no special comment.

JOB DESCRIPTION EXAMPLE 1

Chief Executive ABC plc

Responsible to: Chairman: XYZ Group

Responsible for: Mill Managers (4)
Administration Director
Finance Director
Chief Engineers (4)
Chief Security Officer
Chief Personnel Manager
Liaison/Public Relations Officer

General responsibility:
Subject to the instructions of the XYZ Board, to operate ABC plc with maximum efficiency in terms of output, quality and quantity, costs, machine and manpower utilization and profits, within the plans and budget agreed with chairman XYZ group.

1 Planning

1.1 Annually, obtain draft plans and budgets for their respective areas from immediate subordinates, discuss and agree them provisionally.

1.2 Co-ordinate these into total plans and budget, submit to chairman XYZ group, discuss and finally agree.

1.3 Communicate the agreed plans and budgets to immediate subordinates and instruct them to draft appropriate plans and budgets for their respective areas of responsibility. Discuss these and finally agree them.

1.4 Monitor every month the progress made towards the objectives of these plans and budgets and ensure that any necessary remedial action is taken.

2 Organization
2.1 Decide upon, and implement a management structure and organization to achieve the objectives of the agreed plans and budget, within the capital, revenue and expenditures agreed.

3 Recruitment
Within the general policies laid down by XYZ plc:
3.1 Arrange, through appropriate channels, for advertizing of vacancies in grade D and above, notifying XYZ plc, so that possible candidates from elsewhere in the group may be nominated for consideration. Personally select and appoint staff in grades A and B.

3.2 Decide policies for recruitment of staff in grades C and D and communicate these to subordinates as necessary. Delegate authority to recruit and appoint staff in grades C and D down the management structure as he considers appropriate.

3.3 Cooperate actively in any recruitment activity organized by the XYZ group.

4 Liaison with XYZ Group
4.1 Maintain continuous contact with XYZ group on

    4.1.1 All matters of major policy and especially those which might have effects upon other companies in the group.

    4.1.2 Personal affairs of grade A and B staff. Also of any lower grade staff which cannot be settled satisfactorily within ABC plc.

5 Training and management development
5.1 Train immediate subordinates, in turn, to communicate downward and motivate their subordinates as in 1.3 and 1.4 above.

5.2 Hold a monthly meeting of immediate subordinates to review general performance, to consider future progress and thus to co-ordinate their activities and develop them as managers.

5.3 Every six months (or more frequently for the present) hold a private discussion with each immediate subordinate to discuss progress and problems in his area, using the experience of the past period to improve future performance. Record agreed action as a 'Job improvement programme' for the coming period.

5.4 Train immediate subordinates to delegate decision-making to the lowest possible level which does not involve serious risk of major mis-management.

6 Reporting

6.1 Obtain, from immediate subordinates, the least amount of statistical and other information to permit general (rather than detailed) monitoring of performance in their respective areas.

6.2 Similarly, provide regular returns to XYZ group of overall figures showing progress against agreed plans and targets.

6.3 If requested by XYZ group, provide further detailed information to explain major variations from the agreed plans and budgets.

JOB DESCRIPTION EXAMPLE 2

Job description: Salesman/Trainer

Responsible to: Sales Director

Responsible for: One Salesman and two Trainees

General objectives: Plan, budget and achieve agreed sales and profit targets; supervise training of trainees; carry out development work requested by Sales Director

1 Forecasting

1.1 Prepare sales budget by market areas for each quarter of the financial year, discuss with Sales Director and obtain his agreement.

1.2 Discuss and agree with Sales Director strategies to achieve budgeted turnover and profitability.

1.3 Discuss and agree with Sales Director personal expenditure budget for each market area and key account.

2 Estimates, invoices and results

2.1 Personally check and authorize all estimates and invoices up to £20,000 and within agreed guidelines for the relevant quarter. Submit to Sales Director all estimates and invoices over £20,000 and/or below the agreed profit margin for the relevant quarter.

2.2 Each month, discuss results for each market area and key account with Sales Director. Take agreed action on significant variations and anticipated changes.

2.3 Establish correct reasons for rejected estimates and report to Sales Director. Agree any required action and carry it out.

3 Maintenance and development of customer accounts

3.1 On a planned basis, and also as required by customers' needs, regularly visit and/or telephone customers. Diarize follow-up calls and visits.

3.2 Give technical and other advice when taking orders and involve other members of the company when relevant.

3.3 Each quarter, prepare, and obtain Sales Director's agreement to, entertainment plan.

3.4 Develop existing accounts by gaining introductions to departments and individuals not previously dealt with by the company.

3.5 During visits to customers (see 3.1) check on their plans and any policy changes which may affect their buying decisions. Discuss these with Sales Director, agree upon necessary actions and carry them out.

3.6 Decide, on technical grounds, the group company best suited to undertake any order. In particular, for very specialized work, introduce appropriate group salesman.

3.7 Monitor all the above activities by reviewing each month and reporting to Sales Director, at monthly review (see 2.2 above).

4 Recruitment and training

4.1 As required by Sales Director, interview possible recruits and report views to him, for his decision.

4.2 Identify training needs of new recruits. Plan and implement individual six-month induction programmes.

4.3 After induction period, plan and supervise sales training as required, including sales presentations and techniques, on-the-job practice, joint visits, factory visits and entertaining.

4.4 As requested by Sales Director, advise on training for the sales force, related both to individual and group problems.

4.5 As requested by Sales Director, advise on training required by individuals as revealed by the work review system. Prepare and implement appropriate training programmes.

5 Development work

5.1 As required by Sales Director, investigate growth areas and undertake special projects.

5.2 With agreement of Sales Director, prepare manuals, standard letters, visual aids etc, if appropriate.

6 General management

6.1 Each month, attend sales meeting and departmental management meeting.

6.2 As requested by Sales Director, provide written information for the monthly management meeting.

JOB DESCRIPTION EXAMPLE 3

Job description   Senior Library Assistant

Responsible to   Librarian

General responsibilities   Order library stock and pre-catalogue new material; keep records of expenditure and postal charges; handle and record inter-library loans

Key result areas
1 Ordering books and pamphlets
 1.1 On Librarian's instructions, place orders for all books, government publications etc for library with booksellers and publishers; also order books/pamphlets required by other Departments.

 1.2 On Librarian's instructions, place standing orders; once per month check that all orders have been delivered and follow up any non-deliveries.

 1.3 Before placing order, check against catalogue and existing orders to avoid any duplication; check obscure/inadequate references to obtain more precise details if necessary.

 1.4 Check all new material received against order slips and order-books; deal with any problem arising from errors in supplies.

2 Company material
 2.1 Write to appropriate specialists to ask for copies of company material requested by the Manager or Librarian.

2.2 Update company material by writing to companies nominated by Librarian. Follow up as necessary.

2.3 Prepare and maintain the record of contacts in all companies approached for such material.

3 Pre-cataloguing and filing of catalogue cards

3.1 Prepare material for cataloguing by making a rough slip and checking with previous entries for consistency.

3.2 handle duplicate copies of material by arranging for necessary alterations to be made on the catalogue cards.

3.3 Check filing of catalogue cards done by clerk typist. File catalogue cards in the classified and author/title section after proof reading them against master slips made by the Deputy Librarian.

4 Book expenditure and postal charges

4.1 Maintain record of library book and stationery expenditure by checking invoices upon receipt of items ordered, entering expenditure in library accounts book. Submit invoices to Accounts Department after they are initialled by the Librarian.

4.2 Allocate charges from HMSO and newspaper bills to appropriate departments.

5 Inter-library loans

5.1 Handle applications for and safe return of all material requested on inter-library loans by the Information/Library staff.

5.2 Maintain the record of inter-library loans.

6 Miscellaneous

6.1 Handle overdues (6 weeks or more) by calculating value of material lost and invoicing borrowers.

6.2 Insert received amendments into ongoing reference books and manuals.

JOB DESCRIPTION EXAMPLE 4

Job description   Company Accountant

Responsible to   Deputy Managing Director (Company Secretary)

Responsible for   Management Accountant, Costing Supervisor, Accounts Machine Supervisor, Wages Supervisor, Credit Control Supervisor

General objective   To carry out and/or supervise all costing, accounting, management information services and development of data processing

1 Accounting
 1.1 Ensure that appropriate books and accounts are kept in compliance with company, group and statutory requirements.
 1.2 Ensure that weekly Form X and Time Analysis Sheets are produced accurately and on time, and that the following monthly reports are produced:
  1.2.1 Monthly Form X
  1.2.2 Year-to-date Form Y
  1.2.3 Monthly Non-Chargeable Percentage Summary
 1.3 Ensure that the following are produced accurately and on time:
  1.3.1 Monthly management accounts
  1.3.2 Annual and six-monthly accounts
  1.3.3 Half-yearly stock check and valuation

2 Secretarial duties

2.1 Keep minutes of monthly management meetings.

2.2 Make quarterly and annual statistical returns to DTI.

2.3 Complete year and income tax reconciliations and PIIDs/P9Ds for relevant employees.

2.4 Ensure the prompt and efficient payment of weekly wages and monthly salaries.

3 Costing

3.1 Continuously review the design and effectiveness of the costing system and continuously stress to line managers the need for accurate basic information.

3.2 Ensure that all job cost sheets are sent to Department A no later than five working days after receipt of basic data from Production Office.

3.3 Ensure that all cost queries are answered within four working hours.

3.4 Ensure that Assistant Accountant checks Commercial Manager's estimate of costing margin with Cost of Sales Summary, and checks relevant Summary weekly for additional costs to ensure that all unrecovered costs are identified.

3.5 Ensure that all WIP is accurately recorded in the ledger and at the end of every month computer figures agree with appropriate ledger account.

3.6 In collaboration with Commercial Manager ensure that estimates for all repetitive jobs and those non-repetitive jobs which are estimated are recorded on the cost sheets.

4 Management information services

4.1 Ensure that management accounts and related statistics (eg Computer Sales Analysis and Form Z) are numerically consistent and accurately reflect the financial accounts.

4.2 Ensure that all necessary nominal ledger accounts are analysed up to current month and that capital invoices are extracted separately.

4.3 Ensure that asset records are updated every six months.

4.4 Ensure that the following monthly reports are produced accurately and on time, and monitor their effectiveness.
    4.4.1 Spoilage

    4.4.2 Work in progress over two months old

    4.4.3 Work in progress write-offs

    4.4.4 Outwork Actual/Estimate comparison

4.5 Ensure that Works Director has an accurate aged raw material report each month.

4.6 Co-ordinate the preparation of long term plans.

5 Systems audit

5.1 Ensure that an internal audit is carried out monthly on all raw material stocks and prepare an audit report each month for the management committee.

5.2 Ensure that nominal ledger control accounts are agreed monthly.

5.3 Programme the work of the department and provide and monitor an annual timetable.

5.4 Continuously check that quantitative information issued is appropriate to managers' needs and that guidance is provided with regard to interpretation.

5.5 Continuously review present data processing systems with a view to improving their cost effectiveness.

5.6 With a view to developing data processing facilities in the accounting function make recommendations for extending use of present facilities and, where appropriate, acquisition of improved facilities.

6 General management

6.1 Maximize cash flow by ensuring that:

    6.1.1 Trade debts do not exceed the value of 55 days sales.

    6.1.2 Trade creditors exceed 75 days purchase at any time.

    6.1.3 Ensure the preparation each month of a six monthly cash flow statement and discuss with Deputy Managing Director.

6.2 Develop Corporate Planning System to facilitate budgeting and long term forecasting and improve flexibility of same. Report progress each month to Deputy Managing Director.

7 Budgeting

7.1 Co-ordinate the preparation of the annual budget providing available information as necessary to Sales Director and Works Director. Personally prepare budgeted P&L, Balance Sheet, Cash Flow.

7.2 Co-ordinate the preparation of Company expenditure budget.

7.3 Monitor actual performance against budget throughout the year and provide Management monthly with an analysis of any significant deviations.

8 Other duties

8.1 Ensure that VAT and fire insurance returns, where appropriate, are made for all group companies.

8.2 Training; by implementation of work review system establish needs of each individual subordinate, prepare and implement training programmes accordingly, concentrating where possible on 'on the job' training. Monitor continuously, and also formally at annual work review.

8.3 Personally agree job descriptions for immediate subordinates and ensure that they are kept up to date.

8.4 Recruit subordinates down to grade 3 and authorise recruitment at lower levels.

8.5 Ensure that accurate records are maintained for Company cars and that:
    8.5.1 They are taxed on time

    8.5.2 Any changes are communicated to Group

    8.5.3 A quarterly return is made to Group of Company cars

JOB DESCRIPTION EXAMPLE 5

Job description Salesman

Responsible to Sales Manager

General objective Ensure personal sales targets are met, including key accounts and, especially, XYZ plc

1 Forecasting
Discuss and agree with Sales Manager:
   1.1 Sales budget by market areas, allocated over each quarter of the financial year.

   1.2 Strategy to achieve turnover and profitability.

   1.3 Personal expenditure budget by market areas and key accounts.

2 Results, including estimates and invoices
   2.1 Discuss results, by market area and key accounts, with Sales Manager monthly. Take agreed action on significant variations or anticipated changes.

   2.2 Personally authorize all estimates and invoices up to £10,000 within agreed guidelines for relevant quarters. Refer to Sales Manager all work being quoted or charged below the agreed profit margin for the relevant quarter.

   2.3 Establish correct reasons for each rejected estimate and report to Sales Manager.

3 Maintaining and developing existing business

3.1 Regularly visit and telephone customers as required to meet the customers needs and achieve budgetted sales results. Plan visits to key customers, including other members of the company where relevant. Set and agree an entertainment plan with the Sales Manager. Monitor action taken and review with Sales Manager each month.

3.2 When appropriate, give technical advice when taking an order.

3.3 Develop existing accounts by gaining introductions to new departments and people with whom the company has not dealt previously.

3.4 Keep up to date with customers' plans and policy changes which may influence their buying decisions. Refer any changes to Sales Manager and take necessary agreed action.

3.5 Diarize follow-up calls and visits throughout the year.

3.6 Decide on technical grounds the appropriate group company best suited to undertake an order. Introduce group salesmen to handle very specialized work.

4 New business

4.1 Carry out a credit check through Credit Controller before accepting orders from a new customer.

4.2 Utilize one morning per week telephoning new contacts given by Special Sales Manager. Record action taken on Form MI21 and return to Special Sales Manager.

4.3 Take appropriate action within seven days on leads given by existing customers or sales managers and diarize follow up. During first week of each month, inform Sales Manager of action taken.

4.4 Inform Sales Manager and order controllers of new customers.

5 Communications

5.1 Give full instructions in terms of technical data, changes in job schedules and customer background information, to order controllers and production control.

5.2 Keep customers informed of any changes in schedule or changes from their expectations, including variations to price.

5.3 Inform customers of changes in the company's plant or marketing plans which may affect their buying decisions.

5.4 Inform Sales Manager/Director of any customer comment, especially criticism. In case of production criticism inform the Works Director in writing.

5.5 Continuously inform Sales Secretary of location when away from office.

13

Examples of what to avoid

EXAMPLE 1

This consists of pages three and four of a four page job description for a 'Development Accountant'. It is so long and wordy that it is difficult to get a clear idea of the actual duties involved. It uses vague words and phrases such as 'this involves liaising with'. It combines information about the company's finance and accounting methods with some partial descriptions of the job holder's duties. It is written in the form of a discursive essay and not in terse, active, separated sentences. It lacks subheadings and it does not appear to bring together groups of related topics.

In short, it is a classic case of the trees obscuring the wood.

Nature and scope

The Accounting Development Department has a staff of four in addition to the manager who reports to the Controller Group Accounting who in turn reports to the Group Finance Director.

The development programme is formulated by the Manager Accounting Development in response to internal and external (legislation, exposure drafts, statements of Standard Accounting Practice) forces. The job-holder will be expected to carry out these projects which usually involve working with a Unit Company and liaising with all levels of the accounting function, and could involve the education of the personnel in new systems. Such is the wide ranging nature of development that it can involve a considerable knowledge of subjects outside an accountancy discipline, for example computer software packages.

The major area of development is inflation accounting, which until recently was to be the mainstream accounting system. However, this has been delayed, pending the outcome of the various accounting consultative bodies' opinions of future development. However, the Group still has a heavy commitment, in particular results in current cost terms continue to be published and audited.

The nature of development can be particularly specialized ie applicable to only a limited section of the Group but where there is overall Group potential the job holder will be expected to see such potential and pass on his own experience to other sectors of the Group. This means extensive liaison with Unit Companies (usually Finance Director or Chief Accountant) and departments at Head Office and other development teams.

The job holder performs the duties of Capital Budget Officer who is responsible for the consolidation of capital expenditure information on a quarterly basis for submission to the Group Finance Director. The Capital Budget Officer is expected to appraise the performance of nominated capital expenditure projects which have been recently completed. This involves liaising with the operating management of the project concerned and Corporate Planning and involves a broad commercial judgement rather than a narrow accounting exercise. The report will be submitted ultimately to the Divisional Managing Director.

The job holder prepares, in conjunction with the Assistant Accountant Inflation Accounting, the quarterly and year-end inflation accounts. These accounts must currently be in accordance with the guidelines on inflation accounting and are prepared to meet a tight deadline for inclusion in the published accounts (year-end only) These accounts are subject to audit.

Because of the essentially non-routine function of the Department, it becomes involved in 'one-off' tasks which are not strictly development but are required to be performed.

Such tasks will include acquisition documentation preparation, interim forecasting, consolidation of company plans, integration of new Unit Companies into the Group accounting framework and checking of brokers reports.

The job holder is responsible for keeping abreast of major developments in the accounting field in relation to areas of general management accounting interest which could impact on the Group. This information is discussed within the Department as to the potential for development within the Group and submitted to the Controller Group Accounting for his appraisal.

EXAMPLE 2

This is for a section-leader in an accounts department. It is one page out of *six* pages similar in the complete job description.

The first and third sections are not too bad in some ways. They are itemized and the underlinings of the first two words in each sub-section are partly effective as subheadings although they do not state the content of each section.

However, the writing is more complex than it should be. Phrases like 'thereby determining' are unnecessary. The latter part of sub-section (e) in the first section could, with advantage be shortened to read:

'analyse closing stocks by areas decide values for the Company's final accounts'

This would use 12 words instead of 26 without loss of information and with a great gain in clarity.

The middle section (Staff objectives) is much less satisfactory. The 'Staff objectives' seem to comprise a homily which, however worthy, has no place in a job description. This kind of topic should be part of a training or induction programme.

Means of achieving accounting objectives

The means the postholder uses to achieve the accounting objectives are:
(a) to scrutinize all incoming mail (correspondence, shipping programme, computer tabulations and validities etc), thereby being able to:
  i. allocate priorities to work
  ii. determine in special circumstances how work will be completed
  iii. interpret new contracts
  iv. ensure codes and standing files are promptly updated
  v. check on complaints and alleged errors
(b) to plan from a knowledge of deadlines to be met, from the work on hand and staff availability, how the workload will

be achieved during the next account period or for the next quarterly accounts

(c) <u>to improve</u> the quality of work by investigating errors, resolving difficulties and, where appropriate, devising new procedures

(d) <u>to control</u> the work of staff by countersigning journal vouchers, batch slips, creditors' invoices, payment order, payment credit notes

(e) <u>to prepare</u>/have prepared at the end of each calendar quarter a TOTAL PRODUCT DISPOSAL STATEMENT; and to analyse the closing stocks into the respective stock areas, thereby determining the valuation that shall be placed upon them in the Company's final accounts

(f) <u>to report</u> to the Branch Manager on the progress of work particularly in regard to long overdue accounts, communication problems and other matters that the postholder feels the Branch Manager should be aware of.

Staff objectives

The postholder's duties in relation to staff are those common to any supervisor of a large clerical workforce. He must ensure that his knowledge of all accounting routines is such that he can advise and instruct the members of his team and, when the situation demands, can perform any one of the routines himself. At the same time he must create within the section an atmosphere conducive to the high standard of work required, sometimes under conditions of considerable pressure. He must treat his staff as individuals, attending to their personal difficulties, counselling as required and giving them every opportunity of learning more. When the occasion arises he must formally nominate any member of his section for promotion and reward justly all his staff according to their individual efforts.

Means of achieving staff objectives

The means which the postholder uses to achieve the staff-related objectives are:

(a) <u>to ensure</u> that the lines of communication between the operating departments and his section are well understood and working properly

(b) to plan the staff availability against the expected workload and, in cases of staff absence, to check what work is outstanding and to arrange for its completion as necessary

(c) to train new staff by induction to the industry, the Group's operations and to relate the person's job to the total Trading Accounts contribution: to explain the accounting routines applicable to the person's job and to supervise his work closely for the first two months; to train existing staff by explaining new routines, seeking improvements, giving help and guidance as required

(d) to motivate staff by using their individual abilities, praising effort wherever possible and setting highest personal example

(e) to measure the progress of members of the section, to assess their performance and to report formally to the Branch Manager on an adhoc basis and formally once a year by completing the Staff Review Form.

EXAMPLE 3

This paragraph is from the job description of a 'Financial Controller'. A solid mass of verbiage like this is a thoroughly inefficient way of getting ideas understood. The various items should be grouped, under headings, with spaces. All the abstract nouns (participation, organization, comparison of etc) should be changed into active verbs. Some sentences, eg the last, are too long.

'Responsibilities include participation in corporate strategic planning; the continuous appraisal and interpretation of influences external to the business; the co-ordination of market forecasts, sales objectives and resource allocations into profit plans; as a member of top management, participation in the setting of objectives and the development of policies. Organization of planning and control systems: establishing, administering and developing procedures for resource and expense budgeting, setting of operating standards and standards of performance, appraisal of capital projects and control of subsequent performance. Reporting and interpretation of information for management; data collection, handling and processing; the comparison of performance with plans; communication throughout management of the information necessary for planning, organizing and controlling.

Co-ordination and assessment through managerial controls; as an integral part of top management to co-ordinate and assess managerial performance using budget, performance standards, key result achievement and other appropriate feedback control methods.'

EXAMPLE 4

This job description for a 'Personnel Assistant' is deficient in each of its sections. The first section, 'Function' says nothing and is presumably included because of the ruling that Function must appear. This exemplifies the point made in chapter 2 that nothing is gained by increasing the number of major divisions.

'Position pre-requisite' has no place in a job description. It should (with a simpler title) be in a job specification.

'Responsibilities and authority' has the advantage of being itemized, but lacks headings. Its wording, however, is over-elaborate. Section 3.1, for example, could read:

(1) Organize:
    1.1 factory tours by internal and external parties
    1.2 the work of all guides
    1.3 meetings of outside groups on the Company's premises.

This would use 21 words instead of 47, and be much easier to understand. The only thing omitted is the reference to 'discipline'. This may mean something but conveys nothing as a single word. It should either be omitted or explained.

Finally 'Relationships' makes too much of very little information. 4(a), the upward reporting, is better at the beginning. 4(b) is too vague because 'liaises with' can mean a great deal or nothing. 4(c) is a wordy truism.

Job description—personnel department
Title: Personnel Assistant

1. Function
To assist the Personnel Manager in all aspects of the following duties.

2. Position pre-requisite
Must be a competent typist, who is a self starting type with intelligence and initiative, plus a pleasant personality and the ability to get on with people of all grades and to have received some personnel studies training.

3. **Responsibilities and authority**
    (1) To control the organization of tours of the factory by internal and external parties, and to be responsible for the discipline and organization of the work of the Chief Tours Guide and part-time guides, plus the organization of meetings by outside groups on the Company's premises.

    (2) To carry out surveys of all kinds, concerning employment and welfare conditions, both nationally and locally.

    (3) To liaise with the Personnel Manager in all matters concerning training of Grade 4 personnel and above, to help with the background organization of courses, to issue invitations etc, and to liaise with outside Consultants on courses in the absence of the Personnel Manager.

    (4) To make reservations for all external courses concerning Grades 4 and above, plus arrangements for hotel accommodation, travel and expenses etc, and to pass information on to Statistics Clerks for Training Act recording purposes.

    (5) To be responsible for the booking of the Lecture Room as required by all departments, and for the organization and setting up of internal training courses (TWI etc). Also responsible for obtaining training films either on hire or purchase as requested, arranging showings of training films in the Lecture Room, and passing on necessary information relating to training courses and films to the Statistics Clerks for Training Act recording purposes.

    (6) To be responsible for the recording of all purchasing of literature and books for the Personnel Department and persons attending training courses.

(7) To liaise with the Wages Department on the Company Savings Scheme, issuing information to employees on the scheme and obtaining the necessary forms.

(8) To inform the Wages Department of information with regard to bank accounts of all Grades 4 and above, where necessary.

(9) To take on any projects or enquiries as advised by the Personnel Manager.

(10) To set up and maintain all files appertaining to own work responsibilities.

4. Relationships
   (a) Reports to the Personnel Manager
   (b) Liaises with the Personnel Officer and Safety Officer
   (c) Co-operates with all Senior Management, Departmental Managers and Assistants with whom she comes into contact in the course of her duties.

EXAMPLE 5

This, the job description of a 'Library Clerk Typist', contains too little relevant information and too much which is irrelevant.

The description of 'General responsibilities' is satisfactory. The second section, however, 'Main duties' is quite inadequate, even for a relatively low level clerical job.

Each item raises questions which ought not to arise. These are:

(a) what is 'general library typing'? What is the work, for whom and what standards are required?

(b) What is 'processing'?

(c) What is 'maintaining'? Does the job include selecting the cuttings? If not, where do they come from?

(d) 'Photocopying' what? For whom?

(e) 'Filing' what material? Does the job include up-dating, finding required files or documents?

Section 3, 'Position relationships' is broadly satisfactory. But it is better at the beginning, where it would not need the rather heavy-weight heading. Section 4, 'Qualification' and section 5 'Working conditions' are both out of place in a job description. The former should be in a job specification and the latter in a staff handbook or a letter setting out working conditions.

Library Clerk Typist

1. **General responsibilities**
   Typing and general clerical duties with particular responsibility for the clerical duties involved in adding new books, pamphlets and other materials to the library.

2. **Main duties**
   A wide variety of clerical duties including:
   (a) general library typing
   (b) processing new books and pamphlets

(c) maintaining a press cutting file
(d) photocopying
(e) filing.

3. **Position relationships**
Responsible to the Librarian.

4. **Qualification**
Minimum CSE 1. Typing speed 30–40 wpm accurate. Mature person preferred with ability to work independently under minimum supervision.

5. **Working conditions**
Hours of work: 35 hour week, Monday to Friday. The department operates on a Flexible Working Hours programme. Luncheon vouchers (65p per day) plus morning and afternoon coffee and tea provided by the Company. Contributory pension scheme (contract out).

Index

Accountability 5
Actions 5
Appraisal interviewing *see* Performance review
Aptitudes 12
Authorities 5
Changes—during preparation of job descriptions 1, 3
Communication 30
Company plans 7, 9
Consistency 2, 24–25
Continuing objectives 10, 21
Co-operation 15
Corporate planning, link with 1, 7
Departmental plans 7, 9
Development of staff 1, 9
Discussions during preparation of job descriptions 1, 30–31
Dismissals 2
Drafting 3
Drift 26, 27–28
Duplication 4, 9, 24, 29
Duties 5
Effectiveness 9, 10
Exaggeration 5
Examples,
  satisfactory 30–49
  unsatisfactory 50–61
Flexibility 27

Functional plans 7
Group plans 7
Improved effectiveness 9, 10, 21
Incapability 2, 30–31
Individual tasks 1, 11
Industrial tribunals 2, 30–31
Information, inadequate 15
Job analysis 29
Job evaluation 2, 5, 24, 29
Job grades 1, 6, 12
Job holder 1, 14
Job improvement plan 9
Job specification (*see also* Person specification) 1, 6, 12
Job title 1
Key result areas (KRAs) 1, 6
  content 19
  desirability 18
  examples 18, 34–49
Line managers 3, 10
Management information 19
Management process 7
Managerial responsibility 19
Monitoring 19, 20–21
Morale 13
NIIP 7 point plan 6
Objectives and standards 2, 11, 12
  unclear 15

63

Organization structure   1, 12
Overall purpose   1
Overlap   4, 24–25
Overstatement   5
Performance review   1, 9, 11
Person specification   1, 6
Personal qualities   12
Personality, clashes of   11
    issues   12
Plans   7, 9, 14
Problems,
    joint solution of   1
    raising   15
    resolving   2, 13, 15
Purpose, overall of job   17
Quality of production   19, 21
Quantifying objectives   19
Recruitment   12, 30
Remedial action   19
Repetition   5
Reporting relationships   1, 16–17
Resources, insufficient   15
Responsibilities   5, 17
Salary scales   5
Selection   12, 30
'Selling' to line managers   3
Senior management, role of   1, 14, 15, 25
Separation of areas   5
Setting standards   2, 13
Shop-floor jobs   2, 29

Simplicity, need for   5
Skills   12
Specialists,
    internal or external   24–25
    role of   1, 14, 24–25
Specific objectives   10, 21–23
Standards (of performance)   2, 11, 12
Staff development, link with   1, 9
Strengths and weaknesses   12
Title, job   16
Top level jobs   2
Top management   26–27
Training,
    basis for   1, 12–13
    by whom   14, 24
    job analysis for   29
    need for   2, 15, 24, 30
Updating   10, 27–28
Vagueness   19, 19–20
Value of job descriptions,
    for the individual   13
    for the organization   11–13
Verbiage   5
Work measurement   29
Work objectives and standards   11
Work review   9, 11, 30

How to write a job description

Is concerned with wider issues than the mere writing of job descriptions.

It sees the job description, and the discussions necessary to establish it, as a central and important part of management for more effective performance. It stresses the need for a close association between job descriptions, corporate planning and the process of management development.

Considerable emphasis is placed on the need to 'sell' the process to line managers, and to involve them in drafting and discussions. The author also urges that individuals should draft their own job descriptions and that they should then be discussed with their superiors.

Guidance is given on the need for simplicity, for avoiding vague generalizations, for using straightforward, simple, active phraseology and for setting objective standards wherever possible.

Valuable examples of 'how to do it' and 'how not to do it' are included.

ISBN 0 85292 268 X

Institute of Personnel Management

Cover design Craig Dodd

Edited by
Pamela Abbott and Claire Wallace

Gender, Power & Sexuality